# Black Dahlia

## The Story of America's
## Most Gruesome Murder

Roger Harrington

# Table of Contents

# Prologue

The sun rose over Los Angeles that Wednesday morning in 1947, and a light breeze from the southeast ruffled the hair of Betty Bersinger and her three-year-old as they took a walk down South Norton Avenue in the Leimert Park neighborhood in southern Los Angeles.

It was just two weeks into a new year, January 15, 1947. WWII had been over for almost two years, and dawn was breaking on the cold war. Harry Truman was president. He'd taken charge of the country after Franklin Delano Roosevelt died in 1945, and the country was beginning the push back against the communist ideals of the USSR.

It's a Wonderful Life had just debuted at Christmas 1946, and nobody knew it would grow to be a classic. The Old Lamplighter by Sammy Kaye and his Orchestra was at the top of the Billboard charts, but swing music was on its way out, soon to be replaced by doo-wop, pop, and rock and roll.

Los Angeles was in a real estate boom. G.I.s home from the war were using the new G.I. Bill to buy vacant lots waiting to be transformed into subdivisions with houses to raise the children who would become the Baby Boomers.

Betty Bersinger noticed a white discarded store mannequin laying in a scraggly, undeveloped lot near the side walk; its top half separated from the bottom half.

A closer look revealed two things. The discarded mannequin was actually the naked body of a woman who'd been cut cleanly in half, and the discovery would become one of the grisliest, most notorious murders ever committed in the United States.

It's been 70 years, and still—no one knows who did it.

# Who are you?

Betty ran to a nearby house to phone the police, and LAPD Officers Frank Perkins and Will Fitzgerald arrived at the scene, quickly followed by back up.

Despite the quick police response, the press was faster. Journalists who'd been monitoring police activity via radio descended on the scene and had already begun taking photos by the time officers arrived. One of the first reporters at the scene was the Los Angeles Examiner's Will Fowler and photographer Felix Paegel. It was Fowler who closed the woman's eyes.

Police at the scene noted that the body was lying on its back on the west side of Norton

Avenue with the head to the north and feet to the south. The body was near a paved driveway and just inches from the sidewalk. The two halves of the body were approximately one foot from each other, and the lower half was a foot to the west of the lower half. She had been posed with her hands behind her head and her legs spread.

The grass under the body was wet, meaning she had been placed there after the morning dew had fallen. Rigor mortis had not set in, but there was evidence that she'd been left facedown following her death. Her intestines, protruding from the lower half of her body, were tucked under her buttocks.

The only evidence they really saw was a tire track at the curb.

Meanwhile, the Examiner had the scoop on a hot story and published an early edition two hours before any of the afternoon papers the day the body was found. "Girl tortured and slain: hacked nude body found in LA lot," the main headline screamed with photos of the body (edited to look like it was covered with a sheet) in the center of the front page.

Plans were made to send a copy of the body's fingerprints to the Federal Bureau of Investigation via airmail, but reporters desperate for a story suggested using the paper's new sound photo machine (precursor to the fax machine) to send them quickly. Later, newspapers would report that sending the fingerprints via sound photo was an excellent example of police/media relations.

Fewer than 48 hours after Betty Bersinger's grisly find, the police — and the press — had a name to go with the disfigured face: Elizabeth Short.

The reporters started digging, calling her Elizabeth's mother, Phoebe Mae, and telling her they needed background information because Elizabeth had won a beauty contest.

The heyday of yellow journalism — sensationalizing to the point of lying — was over and the newspaper war between William Randolph Hurst and Joseph Pulitzer had waned, but the Las Angeles Examiner editor had always emphasized that his reporters focus on crime and Hollywood scandal. January 16, 1947 was too early to know for sure, but they were on the cusp of a story that had a little both.

Elizabeth was born on July 29, 1924, to Cleo and Phoebe Mae Short in Hyde Park, Boston, Massachusetts.

Elizabeth—also known as Betty, Bette, or Beth—was the middle child in a set of five sisters. She grew up in Medford, Massachusetts, just three miles northwest of Boston. Medford was quaint—its home to Tufts University and its claim to fame is being the site where Christmas tunes "Over the River and Through the Woods" and "Jingle Bells" were written.

Her father supported the family by building miniature golf courses, though the 1929 stock market crash caused him to lose his money, and he abandoned Phoebe and his five daughters in 1930 when Elizabeth was just six years old. Cleo's car was found on a bridge, and it was assumed he committed suicide until he wrote home to apologize to Phoebe, who'd moved into an apartment and began working as a bookkeeper to provide for the children.

Elizabeth went to see her father in Vallejo, California, when she was 10. The golf mogul was then working at the Mare Island Naval Shipyard.

As a girl, Elizabeth was plagued by breathing trouble, including bouts of bronchitis and asthma, both of which were exacerbated by the frigid Boston winters. At

16 in, her mother sent her to spend the winter in Miami, Florida, something she'd do for three years.

Elizabeth was loved around Medford. A classmate called her a "porcelain Chine doll with beautiful eyes." A neighbor, Dorothy Hernon described her as "good, sweet, funny and not stuck up."

"The truck drivers and men would stare when she walked down the street. It was a wonder there weren't more truck accidents when she walked down Salem Street," Hernon said.

Another neighbor said Elizabeth liked to be admired and called unforgettable, and a third Medford resident said she, Elizabeth, and one of the other Short sisters had plans to be movie stars and talked often of going to Hollywood.

In 1943, Cleo moved some 388 miles south to Los Angeles, and Elizabeth went with him, though her stay was short. Following an argument, she struck out on her own and got a job at the Post Exchange at Camp Cooke, now Vandenburg Air Force Base in Lompoc, California, 150 miles from where her body was found.

Elizabeth's supervisor at Camp Cooke, Inez Keeling characterized Elizabeth as a shy 19-year-old girl. She never smoked and rarely drank, and certainly never spoke to the soldiers, but that changed and she began dating different soldiers several nights a week.

The company she kept got her into trouble of September 1943 when police found her drinking with a group of soldiers at the El Paseo restaurant. She was charged with juvenile delinquency for underage drinking.

She befriended the officer who arrested her, Mary Unefer, and stayed with her for more than a week until she could catch a train back to Massachusetts. Unefer told reporters that Elizabeth had a tattoo of a rose on her leg and she loved to show it off. The officer was positive that Elizabeth had made it home to Medford after her arrest because she'd received letters from her.

Elizabeth didn't stay in Medford long, going back to Florida for a time and spending some time in Chicago as she made her way back west. She returned to California in July 1946 to visit another soldier friend in Long Beach, Lt. Joseph Gordon Fickling. Their relationship was tumultuous. He was soon sent to North Carolina to work as a commercial pilot while she stayed out west. He still sent her money and remained in touch. He received his final letter from her on January 8, a week before she died.

In October 1946, Elizabeth was destitute and living in a Hollywood hotel with two other girls. The girls and their boyfriends went to police after her death, telling them they recognized her as Betty Short, an acquaintance they went to Hollywood night clubs with. The boyfriends recalled allowing Elizabeth to go out with them as the fifth wheel, and they'd pay for her meals because she was "broke and hungry."

The clerk at the Orange Avenue hotel told reporters a "short, dark man" around 35 or 40 years old would pay the bill whenever Elizabeth lagged behind on paying for her room. The man drove a black Ford sedan — which fits the description of a vehicle seen early on the morning Elizabeth's body was found.

When the three girls checked out of the hotel at the end of October that year, they packed their belongings into the short man's dark car. It's possible the man was Mark Hansen, a Danish man who was on the list of likely suspects.

Elizabeth had wanted to become an actress, her mother told the reporters, but later review of records from major movie studios don't list Elizabeth as an extra at any time. In fact, the young woman had recently written home to her mother that she was working at a hospital in San Diego, more than 100 miles from where her body was found.

The details were enough for the paper to nickname Elizabeth "The Black Dahlia," thought to be a play on words of a movie released 9 months earlier—The Blue Dahlia. It was common for reporters to name the grisliest crimes or most depraved criminals. Elizabeth was reportedly known to wear black, and the reporter at the scene noted her hair was dyed black, though her brown roots were showing through. Some accounts said she had friends who called her "The Black Dahlia" long before she was found dead.

A nickname also made it easier to write an attention grabbing, sensationalist headline, something that the paper's editor, James H. Richardson instructed his staff to do.

The Blue Dahlia premiered in April 1946 and told the story of three discharged naval officers who find themselves in Hollywood after WWII. Two of them get an apartment. The third finds out his wife is having an affair with the owner of the Blue Dahlia night club.

The wife ends up dead.

The film had all the elements of the film noir trends of the day — sex, scandal, cynicism and drama.

Information cobbled together by newspaper reporters hot on the trail of the Black Dahlia were able to figure out that she'd last been seen on January 9, a week before her death.

Police talked to Robert "Red" Manley, a former army musician, who said he'd driven Elizabeth from San Diego to Hollywood on January 8. The next day, Elizabeth asked Manley to take her to the Biltmore holiday to meet her sister, Virginia. He dropped her off around 6 p.m. that evening and Elizabeth was spotted making phone calls. It was the last time police could confirm that Elizabeth

had been seen alive.

# Horrors Confirmed

At the scene, police took note of what was nearby before Elizabeth's body was collected and sent for an autopsy.

LAPD Detective Lieutenant Jesse Haskins later described the scene:

"The body was lying with the head towards the north, the feet towards the south, the left leg was five inches west of the sidewalk. . .The body was lying face up and the severed part was jogged over about 10 inches, the upper half of the body from the lower half. . .there was a tire track right up against the curbing and there was what appeared to be a possible bloody heel mark in this tire mark; and on the curbing which is very low there was one spot of blood; and there was an empty paper cement sack lying in the driveway and it also had a spot of blood on it. . .It had been brought there from some other location. . .The body was clean and appeared to have been washed."

There were two cement bags lying near the body, believed to have been used to transport the halves of the woman's body.

Additionally, the woman's face had been slashed into a "Glasgow Smile," a maneuver originated in Glasgow, Scotland in the 1930s. It's a wound caused by slashing the victim from the corners of the mouth towards the ears. Had the woman lived, the scars would have looked like a smile.

Forensic science in the late 1940s was still a burgeoning field. Collecting DNA wasn't an option, and dental records weren't used. Authorities could do only two things: take fingerprints and make observations about the scene and the state of the body before calling the coroner to complete an autopsy.

The results of the autopsy solidified the horror of the barbaric murder.

The surgeon who performed the procedure, Frederick Newbarr, said the Glasgow Smile, extending three inches from each corner of her mouth, would have brought on shock, but Elizabeth would have been alive — and likely conscious — while she was bound and hung upside down.

There were three deep abrasions on Elizabeth's forehead over her right eye, which Newbarr believed were caused by a severe blow with a blunt object. Surprisingly, the hit did not fracture the skull.

Marks from being bound were on her legs, wrists, neck and right thigh, but Newbarr did not find any evidence that Elizabeth had been strangled.

Some accounts say Short had been force-fed feces and had pubic hair and pieces of her own flesh placed into her rectum and vagina. Her uterus was gone.

Officially, the cause of death was shock and hemorrhage, and the surgeon believed she'd been dead for about 10 hours at the time she'd been found.

If any mercy could be found, it was in the fact that she was not cut in half until after she'd already expired.

The killer had removed one of Elizabeth's breasts, and had drained her of blood. The dissection was clean, and the cuts were made just above the waist. None of her organs had been harmed and the cut through her spine was very precise. Her body had been thoroughly cleaned before the killer posed her in the Norton Avenue.

The autopsy also recovered two bristles on her body. One was near the removed breast and the others were among her organs. The

LAPD asked FBI field agent RB Hood to send the fibers to the FBI's Washington technical laboratory for further analysis. He made the request on February 15, and it took five days to get preliminary results back — the bristles were plant fibers of some kind. Further details took until February 26.

The fibers were made of palm trees, the same kind used to produce inexpensive brushes. They were a dull brown, described as stiff, thin and wiry. The bristles had been coated to be water repellent. The laboratory technician believed they came from a cheap brush and invited investigators to send in a whole brush if they ever found one believed to be used on Elizabeth's body.

Phoebe Short and her daughter, Virginia, arrived in California within a few days of receiving the news, but neither one could bring themselves to view the body. Instead, there were plans to get Elizabeth's father, Cleo, who was not speaking to his wife, to identify the body. Accounts vary. Some reports say Cleo couldn't (or wouldn't) view the body either and Phoebe was forced to do it alone.

# Investigation

Police immediately put out an interoffice memo telling officers to search at all hotels, motels, apartment homes, cocktail bars, lounges and nightclubs. There were further details about Elizabeth. The poster called her "very attractive" and noted she had bad teeth and her finger nails were chewed down to the quick.

Red Manley had told police Elizabeth was wearing a black suit with a cardigan style sweater. She was also wearing a fluffy white blouse and suede high-heels and white gloves. She also wore a beige coat and carried a black handbag. In it, police found her address book.

In the days following the grisly find, 50 officers combing the area around the crime scene found no evidence other than a military-type watch. Other officers went to the bars she frequented or to the Biltmore Hotel.

Police put out the all-points bulletin looking for an unidentified Army Lieutenant who Elizabeth had told people she was planning to marry. She was frequently visited by a navy man in San Diego, according to police captain Loren Q. Martin.

Betty Bersinger waited eight days before she spoke with the Examiner on January 24 about finding the body. Bersinger, who lived at 3705 Norton Avenue, was just two blocks from her home when she made the discovery. She said she was shocked and scared and ran to the nearest house — "a doctor's, I think," she told the paper. The home was later identified as that of Dr. Walter Bayley.

The officer who took her call reportedly didn't ask Betty for her name or number, only asking for the phone number she was calling from.

The note with the phone number was reportedly lost for eight days as police had tried to find Bersinger.

By February 25, police were more closely considering the idea that Elizabeth's killer could be in the medical field. They surmised the murder had to have been committed indoors where the killer had access to drains and water because there was no blood found at the scene and the body was very clean from being washed.

"The Los Angeles Police Department has undertaken to develop suspects among the medical and dental schools in the area, as well as other students who have anything to do with anatomy," FBI agent R.B. Hood wrote.

The University of Southern California initially resisted turning over a list of their students without assurance that the names of the students wouldn't be indexed in the case file. They were promised that their identities would be kept private.

Those 300 names were searched through the FBI fingerprint database. It took until March 6 for the search to be complete. It was a dead end.

There were no fingerprints available for 28 of the names. There were many who had non-criminal records of their fingerprints. Three individuals did have criminal records, but nothing that might tie them to the murder.

LAPD Officer Myrl McBride thought Elizabeth looked like a girl she'd spoken with at a bus station on January 14.

"Someone wants to kill me," McBride quoted Elizabeth in the paper.

In a Washington News report dated January 17, 1947, investigators said they were searching for a man who Elizabeth was "deathly afraid of."

When Elizabeth encountered McBride that night, she was sobbing and hysterical, telling the police she needed protection from a jealous ex-marine who wanted to kill her.

She also said she was waiting on the 10:30 p.m. bus from San Diego to meet someone coming to visit.

McBride went with Elizabeth to a bar where she talked to two men and a woman. The officer reportedly told Elizabeth to go home, but she refused, still insisting she had to wait on that bus.

Elizabeth was living with Dorothy French at the time of her death. French said she was "very popular" with men, but one of her dates had her spooked. French also told Examiner reporters that the girl had stored a trunk at a train station in Los Angeles.

The newspaper bargained with the police, saying they'd tell them the location of the trunk so it could be retrieved, as long as the police told the Examiner about the contents so they could print it before the other papers and maintain their lead on the story.

The trunk contained personal items; there was no smoking gun, just more pieces to the puzzle that continued to elude police as leads and tips piled up but did nothing but muddy the water.

Police and reporters recovered lots of clothes and letters from boyfriends. There were photos of Elizabeth with various men, and police started putting names and faces together, but there was one unidentified man.

# Just the Facts, Ma'am

The public was desperate the help solve the crime before someone else got hurt. The Dahlia murder was the fourth unusual case in six weeks, and FBI Field Agent Robert Hood wrote that the citizens were terrorized.

There were two cars seen near the scene — one man reported seeing a Ford sedan stop near the vacant lot around 5:30 the morning Elizabeth's body was found. A different car registered to a man was found at a service station with grass and mud all on its door and hood on the upholstery. Three separate newspapers detailing the crime were on the seat. The car's owner Wilford A. Dougherty lived about six miles from the crime scene. His car was found at a service station nearby.

The FBI files contain a barely legible handwritten letter from January 19. It's from a man in Newark, New Jersey, who wrote to the FBI with a 9-bullet point note of disjointed thoughts. The letter is signed by "Arthur Stange."

He was suggested traits of the killer. Stange said the killer was a white ex-marine between 28 and 30 years old with red hair. The killer was of Irish and English descent and was five-foot, ten-inches tall, and 160 pounds. The writer tells police the check all camps and hospitals in California and writes that the killer can be caught within two weeks.

"I hope you find these help the police," Stange wrote.

The information somewhat matches Robert "Red" Manley, but available records never say if this note enforced their focus on Manley in the days after the murder. Additionally, it is unclear if police ever interviewed Stange to see why a man on the other side of the country believed he had details about the crime.

A letter signed by Edith R. Thomas was sent to J. Edgar Hoover himself on February 15. Her typed note sure had a tale to tell. She believed the murder investigation was being neglected, if not all out staled by the police.

She wrote of hearing a terrible racket coming from the fourth floor of her apartment building at 454 S. Figueroa Street in Los Angeles on January 14, the night before

Elizabeth was found. The resident of Apartment 405? A man named Mr. Hawkins, known as the "old Policeman" by the residents of the building. The tenant in 403 told Thomas she had heard Hawkins yelling obscenities and a woman screaming. The building manager reportedly called the police, and a dozen officers descended on the scene.

Incredibly, the letter goes on to say that police took a bloody Hawkins from the scene and an ambulance came to get the body.

"It was all cut up and terribly mutilated," Thomas wrote. "Her mouth cut from ear to ear."

Thomas did not believe the police were doing anything about it; almost imply they were responsible for dumping the body. She wrote that the women of the building were living in "mortal terror" but were afraid to go to the police because they didn't care.

"The matter is being hushed up," she wrote. "Everybody is afraid of the police."

Hoover wrote back, saying simply, he appreciated her information.

Thomas wrote to Hoover again on February 26 to tell him that the Hawkins man was still living in apartment 405 and that the police and fire department had been there cleaning up after Hawkins. Thomas was still positive that the police were covering up for the man.

Again, Hoover replied to thank her for her information and tell her he would forward her information to the proper authorities.

Case files and news clippings from the day don't seem to make the connection that Thomas's apartment building and the apartment building where suspect Peter Vetcher said Elizabeth lived in September 1946 were just blocks apart.

There is another letter in the FBI file from a few months later. On May 7, 1947, another woman wrote to Hoover. She said the killer was a movie extra and had stolen $70 and her social security number after promising to make her an actress. Her only description of him was that he had a dark complexion, and he was short and thin at five-foot six inches tall and 145 pounds.

Like with Edith Thomas, Hoover simply thanked the letter-writer for her note.

# Similarities and Serial Killers

Just a few weeks after Elizabeth's body was found, there was a second mutilation killing.

On February 10, authorities found the body of Mrs. Jeanne Axford French, 45, a nurse and pilot. Her body was found in the 3200 block of Grandview Boulevard in West Los Angeles, approximately nine miles from where Elizabeth had been found.

She'd been hit with a club and stomped to death by a man's feet, according to the paper. Her body was also discovered naked, and somebody had written "Fuck B.D." on her body in lipstick. Authorities took it as a reference to the Black Dahlia.

Elizabeth's murder was eerily similar to other unsolved sex crimes in San Diego. In the border city, police had already been trying to solve heinous killings for 15 years by the time Elizabeth was killed. They entertained the idea that Elizabeth's killing was the latest and most violent of them.

The San Diego murders had begun 16 years prior when a 10-year-old girl was kidnapped, raped and murdered in February 1931. Three more women were murdered that year, two raped and killed and another stabbed 17 times. The San Diego killer waited three years before striking again and killing another four times. News stories at the time do not mention any similar murders between 1934 and Elizabeth's death in 1947.

Meanwhile, there was another sadistic killer on the loose 2,300 miles away.

Cleveland, Ohio, an industrial city on the banks of Lake Erie, had been tormented throughout the 1930s by a serial killer who murdered and dismembered at least a dozen people in Northeastern, Ohio and Western Pennsylvania.

The victims of the Cleveland Torso Murderer were drifters or the working poor. The torso murderer beheaded all the victims and was killed both men and women. Sometimes he cut the torsos in half like Elizabeth's killer, but in Cleveland, the cause of death was the decapitation or dismemberment. Some victims had some kind of chemical applied to their bodies. The killer often hid the bodies until up to a year or more after their deaths and didn't always return the entire body.

Only two victims were positively identified. The rest are listed only as John or Jane Doe.

And in 1939, the killer claimed there was a Los Angeles victim, but police found only animal bones.

Some crime writers theorize that Elizabeth was killed by the same man who killed six-year-old Chicagoan Suzanne Degnan in 1946. The child was murdered and also dismembered, and some writers have found significance in the fact that Short's Body was found three blocks west of Degnan Boulevard. The notes sent to the newspapers purporting to be from Elizabeth's killer also bore uncanny similarities to the ransom note in Chicago and the newspaper letters from the "Black Dahlia Avenger."

In Chicago, serial killer William Heirens was sentenced to life in prison for killing Degnan. Heirens died at the University of Illinois Medical Center on March 5, 2012, at the age of 83.

# Suspects

## Robert "Red" Manley

Before she arrived at the Biltmore Hotel on January 9, Elizabeth had been leaving in San Diego at Bayview Terrace Apartment. A neighbor there told police she'd gone out with a red head on January 7. She'd reportedly gotten into a car with a sticker that said either Huntington Beach or Huntington Park.

Robert "Red" Manley, the red-headed army-musician-turned-salesman who said he'd dropped Elizabeth off at the Biltmore hotel was arrested on January 19. He was the first person arrested in connection with the murder. He was picked up at a fellow salesman's house, and the authorities impounded his black Studebaker, which he'd stored in another salesman's garage.

Manley was also identified by a Railway Express clerk at the LA station as the man who'd been with Elizabeth when she inquired about shipping a trunk and a suitcase to Ketchikan, Alaska.

Manley was a married man who began seeing Elizabeth in December of 1946. His wife was the same age as Elizabeth—22. Manley was questioned for two hours, and while he admitted he knew the girl, he insisted he had not harmed her.

Manley suggested that a blind date had killed Elizabeth. He said the blind date was a "dark, swarthy" man from San Diego, and that the date had scratched Elizabeth's arms until they bled when he became jealous that she had another date.

Manley's wife and father both said he was home the night of the murder and couldn't have killed Elizabeth.

A January 19 Washington Post article, however, puts Short at a drive-in restaurant near San Diego the day before her mutilated body was found. A waitress in San Diego told police she served Elizabeth and Manley on January 14 at the restaurant.

Manley insisted police allow him to take a lie detector test, and he passed it twice. His release from custody left police at somewhat of a dead end, so they considered some alternative possibilities.

A January 18 article quoted the police psychiatrist as saying the killer was a "sex-perverted madman" or more specifically, the murder was, "plainly the work of a sex maniac manifesting 'the sadistic component of a sado-masochist complex.'"

Police went so far as to consider that a woman had committed the crime. They were pushed by two things: Elizabeth didn't have any luggage with her the last time she'd been seen on January 9, and there were some similarities between her murder the murders of other people that had been committed by women. They went down the female killer rabbit hole after clearing Manley of any wrongdoing.

The papers read like a witch hunt as police sought to find the killer. The homicide squad was mostly new at the time Elizabeth's body was found. The men were inexperienced and transferred into the unit from other areas of police work. The slow moving investigation was mentioned in a February 20 interoffice memo and hinted around at the fact that Los Angeles Mayor Fletcher Bowron was desperate to have the case solved — desperate enough he wanted to involve the FBI as an investigating agency despite the fact they didn't have jurisdiction.

The LAPD was so desperate to find the killer; they even arrested a man who'd been mumbling in his sleep. Glen Thorpe, 32, had said, "I forgot to cut the scar off her leg." Police found him to have an airtight alibi.

The Press, while sensationalizing the case, jeopardized it according to the letter because they had already disturbed the scene and taken evidence before officers arrived. That with their publishing of tell-all reports with key witnesses had undoubtedly harmed the investigation.

"Reporters are in the offices of the Detective Bureau and it is not possible for the investigators to have a confidential telephone conversation or even read mail without having some news reporter looking it over to see if it relates to this case," Hood wrote.

## Peter Vetcher

Army Sergeant Peter Vetcher quickly emerged as a potential likely suspect when police found his name in Elizabeth's address book. As an added point of intrigue, police believed the pair had been married according to a September 1946 postcard that Elizabeth had signed, Elizabeth Short Vetcher.

Vetcher was an Army Ranger, and he'd been captured in Italy by the Nazis on January 30, 1944. He was held in captivity at the Stalag 3B prisoner of war camp in Fuerstenberg, Prussia (now Eisenhüttenstadt, Germany, on the border with Poland). His captivity lasted until July 9, 1945

Stateside, Vetcher's job with the army was to collect AWOL and deserter soldiers back to Fort McClellan, Alabama, and he was in Los Angeles September 20, 1946, to look for fugitive soldiers.

Vetcher told police he was leaning against a wall at the corner of Sixth and Olive Streets in Downtown Los Angeles when Elizabeth and another young woman walked by around 2 p.m. Elizabeth noticed the first ranger battalion insignia on his khaki uniform. She asked if he knew John O'Neil — she'd seen the same insignia on his uniform.

Following the amicable conversation, Vetcher asked Short on a date, and she agreed. She told him her name was Betty and that she was living at the Figuearoa Hotel with another young woman.

On their date that night, Vetcher and Elizabeth saw a Tony Martin broadcast and ate at Tom Brenneman's restaurant. Vetcher recalled that Elizabeth seemed to be well-known at the establishment. They hadn't had to wait for a table despite the long line, and the wait staff seemed to know her.

The soldier recalled a mysterious happening as he and Elizabeth headed back to the hotel — when they debarked from the trolley and began walking to the hotel, a black car pulled up beside them and stopped. The car had five men in it — Vetcher believed they were Mexican — and three of them exited the car yelling "There she is!" Vetcher didn't think Elizabeth knew them.

Once in the room, Vetcher said he and Elizabeth had sex multiple times throughout the night, but that "at no time was the victim in a passionate mood."

Vetcher, however, told police that they were never married; instead, they were playing a joke on O'Neil.

"It was on September 21 when the discussion of O'Neil came up that the victim stated that she had formerly gone with him and he was quite jealous of her and to play a joke on O'Neil she suggested that they both send postcards to him informing O'Neil that she was married to Vetcher," said a newspaper report at the time.

Vetcher, Elizabeth, her roommate, and another man went on a double date on September 21. As the women went into the lobby, Vetcher told police he saw Elizabeth arguing with a "short, chunky, well-dressed man." He was probably 40-45 years old.

It was the last time Vetcher saw Elizabeth alive.

Vetcher had contacted the LAPD after reading about Short's murder because he feared his name would appear in her address book as she'd promised to write to him while he was at Fort McClellan.

The investigation revealed that Vetcher had been assigned to Camp McClellan outside of Anniston, Alabama, on July 19, 1946 and was there until January 28, 13 days after Elizabeth's body was found. His most recent furlough had been for a couple weeks in August 1946.

### Leslie Dillon/Jeff Connors

Almost two years after the murder, LAPD psychiatrist J. Paul De River received a letter from 27-year-old Leslie Dillon, in October 1948.

Dillon, who'd previously lived in Los Angeles, was writing from Florida. He had gone to De River about possibly collaborating on a book about the case because he was interested in psychopathic cases, sadism and sexual vagaries. De River reportedly said Dillon knew more about sadism and psychiatry than he did.

Dillon, who was working as a bellhop, had aspirations to be a writer and had been a mortician's assistant at one time.

Dillon was a Navy man, according to the Washington DC Evening Star, and another paper reported he'd been discharged "irregularly" from the Navy after he was arrested in San Francisco for pandering in 1946.

He had other aliases — Jack Sands and JF Dillon.

Most of all, LAPD Chief CB Horall said Dillon knew too much about the crime, "which could be known only to a person with direct knowledge of the murder itself."

The Washington News called Dillon the "best suspect yet," following his arrest on January 11, 1949.

Prior to the arrest, an undercover LAPD officer and Dr. De River met him in San Francisco where they talked at length about the crime. Dillon named his friend, Jeff Connors, as the true murderer, De River entertained the idea the Connors was a figment of Dillon's imagination.

Eventually, the three made their way to Los Angeles together by car, and the undercover officer posing as a chauffer drove into the area where the body was dumped as they headed for Dr. De River's office.

Dillon, however, kept telling the driver what alleys and side streets he could and could not get through. In time, they made it to the scene and Dr. De River directed the drive to stop.

Later, the undercover cop said Dillon became agitated and nervous while they lingered at the scene.

De River also recorded his conversations with Dillon, and he asked Dillon what he thought the killer would have done with the pubic hair shaved from the body and the tattoo cut from the leg.

Dillon told the doctor he thought the killer would have flushed it down the toilet.

The doctor and the undercover officer drove their suspect from Los Angeles to San Francisco in search of Connors.

Dillon was arrested when they didn't find the other man, though Police quickly learned Connors did exist.

Connors, according to Dillon, knew specific details about Elizabeth's murder, and police questioned him in January 1949.

40-year-old Connors, whose real name was Arthur H. Lane, told police he'd been working at Columbia Pictures as an extra with his ex-wife, Vicki Evans, the night of the murder. He also told authorities that Evans's real name was, Grace Allen.

Connors said he knew Elizabeth Short "by sight" and that he and a girlfriend had seen her in a bar the night before she was killed.

Further investigation revealed that actress Vicki Lane had no idea who Arthur Lane was, declaring she'd "never seen the jerk." Connors did, however, have an actual ex-wife whose name was Grace Allen.

Allen said Connors was working, but said she had no idea why he was using a stage name or why he said his ex-wife was Vicki Evans.

Columbia pictures had no records of Connors or Lane on their payroll.

When Dillon was finally released from jail, he filed a $100,000 lawsuit against the city of Los Angeles. Adjusted for inflation, that would be a $1.1 million suit today. The suit, however, was dropped when it came out that Dillon was a suspect in a hotel robbery in Santa Monica.

He was eventually considered by a grand jury in Elizabeth's, but he was never indicted. The case was circumstantial — he was interested in the types of cases, he knew his way around a body because of his work at the funeral home, and he knew details about the crime, but that wasn't enough to take to trial. Second, he'd been illegally detained by the police, and there were at least a handful of people who said they'd seen Dillon in San Francisco during the time that Elizabeth was murdered. By February 1951, Dillon's name didn't even appear on a list of suspects compiled by the district attorney's office.

## Mark Hansen

Some theorists believe that Mark Hansen, who immigrated from Denmark in 1919, was the killer.

In America, he first lived in Plenty Wood, Montana, eventually moving to the Los Angeles area in 1921 where he owned nightclubs and theatres, and some accounts say Elizabeth was a waitress in one of his establishments.

Records form the time described 55 years old and 175 pounds. He was approximately five-foot, nine-inches tall, but he was said to walk somewhat stooped over.

Actress Ann Toth and Elizabeth shared a room near Hansen's Florentine Gardens night club. Accounts vary, but one of the women was dating Hansen.

Elizabeth had mentioned to Toth that Hansen was a jealous man with a temper, and some accounts say Elizabeth moved in and out of Hansen's house several times in the fall of 1946. Elizabeth also told Toth that she'd had to rebuff Hansen's sexual advances and avoid letting him see her boyfriends.

According to the DA file, Hansen last saw Short alive on December 6, 1946, when they went out to dinner and then to a hotel. The night went poorly, according to the file, and Elizabeth cried and said she was leaving to go see her sister in Oakland.

Elizabeth did go back to San Diego, and she evidently called Hansen to ask if she could come home on January 8 prior to catching a ride back to Los Angeles with Peter Vetcher. The file from the DA says Hansen gave contradictory statements about what he said when Elizabeth called. He initially told Ann that he told her he could come home. He told police that he told Elizabeth she couldn't stay because Ann wouldn't like it.

Ann reportedly had a boyfriend of her own, Leo Hymes.

A file from the district attorney's office noted that Elizabeth had called Hansen again from the Biltmore the night of January 9 before she walked outside and headed down Olive Street.

"In the statement he [Hansen] says victim could have phoned him the night she disappeared at the Biltmore Hotel as he admits getting a phone call and tells a different story about his conversation with her than the story he originally told Ann Toth at the time of the murder. Ann had been living with him sometime prior and sometime after the murder, he told her that victim phoned and asked to come back and live [with] him and he said that he victim, "Ok, come and stay with me until you can find some other place." He told police and undersigned that he said to her, "You cannot come to stay with me because Ann is not here and she would not like it," the DA's account read.

After Elizabeth's body was found, Toth and Hansen willingly went to the police department to give a statement, though both were adamant that their privacy be respected as they wanted to avoid the media circus outside.

When the Los Angeles Examiner received the envelope with Elizabeth's things on January 24, 1947, they received a piece of evidence linking Hansen to Elizabeth. His address book with his name embossed in gold on the front was one of the items. Elizabeth had swiped it from his home and had been using it. He told authorities it had been sent to him from Denmark and he had no idea she had it.

According to the DA file, none of Hansen's Los Angeles properties were ever checked for the presence of blood. Hansen was still considered a prime suspect when the grand jury convened in 1949, though they never issued an indictment.

Other than being investigated when Elizabeth's body was found, he had no criminal record and wasn't known to be physically violent.

In a strange coincidence, Hansen himself almost became a victim of murder in 1949 when a taxi driver/dancer named Lola Titus shot him at his Carlos Avenue home. The bullet ripped through his lung and missed his heart by millimeters. If Hansen was jealous and determined to be with Elizabeth, then Titus was just as dedicated to Hansen.

"I made up my mind that he was either going to love me, marry me or take care of me or I was going to kill him," she was quoted as saying.

## Patrick S. O'Reilly, M.D.

As the investigation went on, police considered a medical doctor who seemed to meet all the criteria of someone who could have been responsible for killing Elizabeth.

Dr. Patrick S. O'Reilly was a friend of Mark Hansen and frequently spent time at the Florentine Gardens.

He was rumored to enjoy wild sex parties in Malibu, and he'd once been married to the daughter of a retired Los Angeles Police Department captain. Their marriage ended in divorce.

According to the DA files, O'Reilly had violent tendencies. He had been convicted of assault with a deadly weapon after he took his secretary to a hotel and beat her "for no other reason than to satisfy his sexual desires without intercourse," the file said.

For reasons not outlined in the file, O'Reilly's right pectoral muscle had been surgically removed. Had he killed Elizabeth and hinted at his identity by also removing her breast?

## George Hodel

Another physician, George Hill Hodel Jr., who specialized in public health and sexually transmitted diseases, first caught the eye of police in 1949 when his teenaged daughter said he'd raped her.

Hodel was the only son of Russian-Jewish parents and was considered a musical prodigy, playing concert halls in Los Angeles. Piano composer Rachmaninoff reportedly once came to hear him play. As an adult, he ran with Los Angeles socialites like director John Huston and photographer Man Ray.

Authorities placed Hodel under surveillance for more than a month in 1950, and they captured several incriminating statements via the microphones placed in his home. At the time, eighteen detectives were reportedly assigned to monitor the microphones in multi-hour shifts. Conversations reportedly revealed references to illegal abortions, police bribery and references to murder.

"Supposing' I did kill the Black Dahlia. They couldn't prove it now. They can't talk to my secretary anymore because she's dead.... They thought there was something fishy. Anyway, now they may have figured it out. Killed her. Maybe I did kill my secretary," Hodel said on the first day his home was bugged.

Hodel's secretary, Ruth Spaulding, had died of an overdose in 1945. Hodel was questioned then, but the case was dropped because of the lack of evidence.

According to the grand jury file, police later discovered documents that indicated the secretary had planned to blow the whistle on Hodel's fraud scheme where he misdiagnosed patients to overcharge them for unnecessary medications and testing.

According to the DA's file, a Lillian DeNorak who lived with the doctor told authorities he spent time at the Biltmore Hotel and identified Short as a girlfriend of the doctor. DeNorak was later committed to the State Mental Institution, though the DA file does not say why.

Tamar Hodel told authorities said her mother, Dorothy, heard her father say, "They'll never be able to prove I did that murder."

A boarder at the Hodel home cooperated with police and handed over a photo of a nude Hodel with a nude woman, later identified as a model. The model could not connect Hodel to Elizabeth. Another man who knew both Hodel and Elizabeth didn't believe they'd ever met.

According to the DA file, police questioned around a dozen of Hodel's acquaintances, but none of them could link Hodel to the murder.

Yet even Hodel's own son, Steve Hodel, believes his father did it.

Steve Hodel is a former LAPD homicide detective and the author of a book, Black Dahlia Avenger: A Genius for Murder that claims his father had killed Elizabeth as well as several other women over the course of 20 years.

Steve Hodel came to believe his father was responsible for the murder after the elder Hodel's death in 1999. Among his personal items were photos of a woman who resembles Elizabeth, although surviving Short family members deny it is her.

Steve Hodel has several reasons for believing his father is the killer. The car spotted near the scene was consistent with the one his father drove. The handwriting on the notes sent to police and newspapers were nearly identical to his father's.

Hodel left the country in 1950 and didn't return until 1990. He died of heart failure in 1999.

In a shocking turn of events, the LAPD announced in 2004 that all the physical evidence in the Dahlia case was missing. The evidence, which would have consisted of Elizabeth's address book, her purse and shoes, the notes mailed by the "Black Dahlia Avenger," the man's watch, hair follicles, and finger print cards, is all missing. By 2004, science had advanced enough that making a DNA match to the elder Hodel would have been possible and the case could have been put to bed once and for all.

In 2014, there were soil analysis tests completed at the home Hodel lived in from 1945 to 1950. The soil samples had evidence of human remains.

Once the book was published, Deputy District Attorney Stephen Kay proclaimed the case solved (the investigation does remain open) and said he'd charge George Hodel with murder if he was still alive.

Steve Hodel went on to link his father to other killings, even surmising he could be the Zodiac Killer. His research has morphed into four books and a lively website where he continues to update the blog almost daily.

## Walter Bayley

Dr. Walter A. Bayley was a 67-year-old WWI veteran who lived in the home just south of the lot where Elizabeth's body was found — or at least, he lived there until he divorced his wife in October 1946. She still lived there when Betty Bersinger came to use the phone and call for police. His name is not in case files and he was never considered a formal suspect by authorities or the grand jury. His name didn't even surface until the late 1990s when a Los Angeles Times copy-editor began working on a piece for the 50th anniversary of Elizabeth's murder.

Some Black Dahlia experts have linked Bayley to short by way of the physician's daughter. The daughter was reportedly a friend of Elizabeth's sister, Virginia — the same sister she was supposed to meet on January 9 when Peter Vetcher left her at the Biltmore Hotel.

Bayley died in 1948 of natural causes. An autopsy revealed he was suffering some kind of neurological deterioration.

Critics questioned the copy-editor's theory. How could an old man with a failing brain commit something so horrific?

The mental deterioration could have caused an otherwise docile person to become violent, and Bayley's medical specialties included mastectomies, removal of fat, and hysterectomies.

An FBI profiler said the location where Elizabeth was posed had to have had some kind of significance to the killer, and he believed the facial lacerations indicated anger towards Elizabeth, and the profiler thought Elizabeth's tendency to lie about losing a son would have angered Bayley, whose son died when he was hit by a car.

The son's birthday was January 13, just two days before Elizabeth's body was discovered.

**Ed Burns**

An even wilder theory is that Elizabeth was killed by a boyfriend and staged as a mockery of the Degnan case.

The name Ed Burns appears in few places online. One is a website done as a class project. That site sends readers right back to the Black Dahlia Solution website.

The site has zero information about the author; though searching for the domain registry reveals it belongs to a man in New Hampshire with the initials J.D.

His theory is this:

The unidentified man in the photo from Elizabeth's trunk is of Ed Burns, and Ed Burns was actually Maurice Clement in the district attorney's suspect list.

Elizabeth, who'd spent a short amount of time in Chicago, was fascinated with the

Degnan case. Some accounts say she masqueraded around the Windy City saying she was a reporter from Boston, and she loved to tell other bar patrons all the grisly details she'd read in the papers.

She headed back west again and met Ed Burns in Los Angeles. Ed Burns had a few credits from a stint at the University of Southern California Medical School. (It's unknown if he was ever on the radar with police first asked for records from there in 1947.)

Burns and Elizabeth often met in Hollywood, according to J.D., and Burns loved Elizabeth even though she didn't exactly return his affections. J.D. implies that Elizabeth used Burns. He could bail her out of trouble with food and rent money. Meanwhile, she'd stay the night with him occasionally, always ducking attempts at being a couple.

J.D. also believes Elizabeth's obsession with the Degnan case and her repeated rejection of Burns caused him to snap.

When Burns snapped, he did to Elizabeth what Heirens did to Degman: both were cut into pieces, both had their hair shampooed. There were patches of crisscross scratches cut into Elizabeth in direct opposition to the gauze Heirens put on his victim's fatal wounds. J.D. claims Burns made Elizabeth eat feces much like Heirens defecated on his victims.

J.D.'s theory is that Burns sent the letters to the police and newspapers, and that they're a cipher with hidden clues throughout.

He definitely believes dumping the body near Degnan Boulevard was no coincidence; it was all part of Burn's master plan.

Burns committed suicide on March 14, 1947; two months after Betty Bersinger found Elizabeth's body.

The note he left said, "To Whom It May Concern: I have waited for the police to capture me for the Black Dahlia killing, but have not. I am too much of a coward to turn myself in, so this is the best way out for me. I couldn't help myself for that, or this, Sorry, Mary."

J.D. believes the suicide note is also a cipher, but he also believes the LAPD knew it was Burns.

So why not prosecute? He says it's because the case had already drawn so much attention that there would have been no way for the police to tell the public that their killer was already dead and deprive them of parading a sadist through the courts and sending him to prison.

J.D.'s website is blackdahliasolution.org.

## Famous Suspects

At least three well-known people were accused of the crime.

Gangster Benjamin "Bugsy" Siegal was suspected of the killing, though the exact reason why was unclear. It was common knowledge at the time that Bugsy was more concerned with loose women and a Las Vegas hotel and casino.

Filmmaker Orson Welles was named as a suspect by a former Short family neighbor, Mary Pacios. Pacios claimed Welles had "practiced" the murder on mannequins that bore almost identical lacerations to Elizabeth.

Additionally, Pacios believed Welles was familiar with the Norton Avenue area and that he was acting out a magic trick he had performed for soldiers during WWII.

Witnesses Pacios talked reportedly believed they'd seen Welles and Elizabeth. Pacios also pointed out the fact that Welles applied for a passport the same day the newspaper received the packet of Elizabeth's belongings. Welles went on to stay in Europe for 10 months.

Welles was never mentioned as a suspect in the official investigation.

Folk singer Woodie Guthrie was even fingered as a potential suspect. A 2004 biography said Guthrie was scrutinized after sending explicit letters and newspaper clippings to a woman he was reported to be stalking. He was quickly cleared of any wrongdoing in the case.

# I Confess

On January 24, the Los Angeles Examiner received its first communication from someone purporting to big the killer. It was a sheet of paper covered in words cut from newspapers. It said, "Here is Dahlia's belongings. Letter to Follow."

The envelope was addressed to the Examiner and other papers, but we delivered to the Examiner. It contained her address book and birth certificate, according to a report in the Washington Times.

Another note said that the killer would give himself up on January 29 at 10 a.m. That deadline came and went, and this time, authorities received another letter. It said "I have changed my mind about surrendering. I'm afraid I wouldn't get a fair deal."

A day later, Elizabeth's shoes and purse were found in a dumpster.

Within six days, there had been several more notes purported to be from the killer, but the authenticity of them has been questioned since they were initially received.

Daniel S. Vorhees, 33, was one of the first confessors. The Washington News first reported it on January 28, 1947. Police, however, called him "addled" and noted that he could not seem to remember when he joined the army — telling police he joined in both 1941 and 1943.

Vorhees said he dated Elizabeth in 1941 and then took her on a date the day of the murder.

He had allegedly called police to confess and offered a note saying, "I did kill Beth Short."

His confession was quickly discounted.

In early February 1947, Army Corporal Joseph Dumais of Fort Dix, New Jersey, said it was "possible" he was the Black Dahlia killer after he was arrested for refusing to return money he had held onto for another soldier. The newspaper report said he had a "woman-beating past."

The army, however, refused to give interviews or allow the press to talk to

Dumais. There was a large weakness in the case – records showed that Dumais was in New Jersey on the afternoon of January 15, the day the body was found.

Dumais said he had been on a date with Elizabeth, but then his mind went blank and he didn't remember anything until he found himself at Penn Station in New York City. The man was examined by a psychiatrist who recommended he be hospitalized. Dumais was found to be carrying clippings about the murder, and there was human blood stained on the pocket of his pants.

Capt. Jack Donahoe, head of the LA homicide squad, said the only way Dumais could have done it would have been if he dropped the body on the night of January 14 and then took a constellation plane back east.

Sergeants at the base said they saw Dumais on January 10 following a 45-day furlough, and they saw him again on January 13, 14, and 15. Records indicate he was there on January 12, but it was unclear where he was on January 11. Dumais also told police that his first wife died under mysterious circumstances, though further investigation found her to be alive and well in Tilton, N.H.

Additionally, five enlisted men could provide alibis for Dumais; they had seen him on the base and remembered him specifically because he was reprimanded for wearing the uniform of a counter-intelligence officer.

In March of 1947, 23-year-old Melvin Bailey from Lemay, Missouri, was arrested on an auto theft charge when he confessed to killing the Black Dahlia.

Bailey claimed he was taking Benzedrine, an amphetamine, and didn't remember much, but he did tell police he used his commando knife to cut Elizabeth up on January 14. The two had been drinking in Los Angeles and were planning to head back to Missouri when Elizabeth said she would be making the trip with two soldiers instead.

Police said his timeline was off because he said he killed Short long before the evening of January 14, which is when the autopsy estimated she had been killed.

A year after Elizabeth's body was found, a 23-year-old painter named Charles Lynch confessed to police, saying he was under the influence of marijuana and "hacked her to pieces with a surgical knife."

Lynch said he knew Elizabeth from a café near Camp Cooke where she had worked as a waitress. He said their paths crossed again on January 14 in a bar. Lynch said they went to a hotel and smoked some marijuana.

"We took off our clothes and I killed her with a surgical knife I stole from the Camp Cooke hospital while I was in service," he was quoted as saying.

His alleged method of murder did not match the autopsy results.

There were even two confessions from women. A 24-year-old woman named Emily E. Williams claimed the shot and stabbed Elizabeth in an auto court outside LA. Police believed she was suffering from mental illness.

The other female confession came from Mannie Sepulvada to called police to say she'd committed the crime. After they questioned her, they determined she knew nothing about the crime.

Three years after the murder, in 1950, an inmate from the Danbury Correctional Institution in Connecticut wrote to say that the killer was a fellow inmate. The letter writer said the murderer was a "Spanish fellow from Puerto Rico named Fredy."

Almost 9 years after the crime, Ralph Von Hiltz, 44, walked into a police station and told the lieutenant at the desk that he wanted to surrender. They'd first talked to him around January 18, 1947, after Elizabeth's murder.

"He was a friend of a red-headed sailor named Daniel James, who was stationed at the San. Diego, Calif., Naval Base. The movie struck Short girl whose home was in Medford, Mass., was keeping company with the sailor," they Journal American had written in 1947.

Von Hiltz told police that he met Daniel James in Los Angeles the night of the murder and they went to pick Elizabeth up. James accused her of seeing another man, and when she got out of the car, Von Hiltz said James shot her in the stomach with a .22 caliber semi-automatic gun.

Von Hiltz went on to tell police that James demanded he cut her up, so he did. He said he never implicated James because the man was known to carry a gun.

# The Grand Jury and the Cover up

While the Los Angeles Examiner had been hot on the story, the other LA papers weren't far behind.

Over at The Herald Express, Agness "Aggie" Underwood had already been a woman in a man's world for twelve years the morning Elizabeth's body was found.

It was Aggie who first interviewed Red Manley, but the morning her story ran, she was pulled from the case. Two days later she was back on the story before being removed permanently and put on the city desk instead.

Some Black Dahlia scholars believe it was all part of a cover up. If the LAPD was trying to protect the killer, the promotion to city editor was a great way to keep her from following the story.

Two years later with no end to the case in site and the best suspect untouchable because of police misconduct, a 21-member grand jury was convened to investigate the facts surrounding the crime.

Normally, a grand jury decides whether or not the police have probable cause to indict and take someone to trial, but grand juries also have the authority to investigate crimes or community issues and make recommendations with their findings.

While the jury didn't have a suspect to indict in Elizabeth's case, they agreed that Leslie Dillon was the prime suspect. They also found the crime scene, according to a September 1949 article in the Washington Times Herald.

The scene was described as house on one of LA's busiest streets just 15 minutes from the lot where her body was found. "Blood-covered sheets and blood-stained clothes of the size worn by the Black Dahlia were seen in the room." the paper reported grand jury investigators as saying. The article in the FBI files never gave an exact location of the crime scene.

The grand jury also looked into whether or not there was police corruption within the

LAPD. Once its investigation was done, the jury issued a report that said this in part:

"Deplorable conditions indicating corrupt practices and misconduct by some members of the law enforcement agencies in the county… alarming increase in the number of unsolved murders… jurisdictional disputes and jealousies among law enforcement agencies."

The report revealed that there was infighting at the department, which caused vital case information to be withheld between the officers. The revelation shook the entire system and ended in the resignation of the police chief.

# The Black Dahlia in pop culture

Perhaps the only way Hollywood could make sense of the slaying in its backyard was to try processing it through art. The fascination with Elizabeth has spawned several movies and a few short stories.

The novel True Confessions by John Gregory Dunne was inspired by Elizabeth's death. It was adapted into a movie of the same name starring Robert De Niro and Robert Duvall.

James Ellroy, a US crime fiction writer, wrote a fictionalized version of the case in his book, The Black Dahlia.

A short story penned by Joyce Carol Oates won the Horror Writers of America Bram Stoker Award for "Black Dahlia and White Rose," a multiple-narrator account of the murder.

There's a film called, "The Black Dahlia," though its plot has nothing to do with Elizabeth's case.

The story has also been rehashed multiple times in books and in television specials about unsolved crimes. America's Most Wanted even made a plea in 2006 asking for the return of evidence missing from the LAPD storage locker.

# Today

The case is still open according to the LAPD, and there is still a list of potential suspects, though most of them have died. It's up to people with a fascination with the macabre to make their own summations about who killed Elizabeth and whether or not there was police misconduct.

Death records for Leslie Dillon could not be immediately ascertained, but if he was 27 in 1947, he was born around 1920. If he was still alive, he'd be 93 in 2017.

Red Manley was eventually committed to a mental institution after suffering from a series of nervous breakdowns. He died January 16, 1986 after an accidental fall.

Mark Hansen died June 14, 1964, of natural causes without ever facing any charges. All of his theatres and nightclubs are closed except for the Florentine Gardens, which still stands on Hollywood Boulevard.

The Biltmore Hotel is now the Millennium Biltmore Hotel and remodeling has taken it from 1500 guestrooms down to 683. It's a popular place to filming movies and television, including the music video to Thinking Out Loud by Ed Sheeran and TV scenes from Columbo, NYPD Blue, Mad Men, and CSI: New York

Initially, Phoebe Short told reporters she'd bring Elizabeth buried in the Mountain View Cemetery in Oakland, California, almost 400 miles from Leimert Park. A flat, rectangular stone marks her gravesite, saying simply,

"Daughter

Elizabeth Short

July 29, 1924 – Jan. 15, 1947."

She's buried in the northeast end of the cemetery near the fourth fountain along the main drive. Her mother, Phoebe, moved Oakland to live near her daughter's grave. Phoebe passed away in Vero Beach, Florida, in 1992.

Elizabeth's childhood home at 115 Salem Street in Medford is now the site of a freeway exit roundabout. A memorial plaque stands nearby, erected by the Medford Historical Society in 1993.

Robert "Red" Manley was committed to a mental hospital in 1954 and eventually died on January 9, 1986, 39 years to the day that he'd dropped Elizabeth off at the Biltmore Hotel.

January 9, 2017, marked the 70th anniversary of Elizabeth's death. The empty, undeveloped lot she was found on is now the site of a two-bedroom home on a neat street of tract houses. Leimert Park became known as a center for African-American art, culture and Music in the Los Angeles area.

The Los Angeles Examiner eventually became the Los Angeles Herald-Examiner and was shuttered in 1989. The remaining Los Angeles newspapers didn't report on the 70th anniversary. The LA Times hasn't written anything about Elizabeth since 2014. The BBC posted a short article commemorating the anniversary, noting that the Biltmore Hotel is where to find a Black Dahlia cocktail consisting of vodka, Chambord black raspberry liqueur, and Kahlua.

Elizabeth's story is an extreme telling of a story so common—a dreamer leaves home and heads west, hoping to make it big only to have his or her dreams dashed and mutilated. She wanted to be remembered; she wanted to be known.

Elizabeth craved fame.

It wasn't the way she planned, but she got it.

Made in the USA
Middletown, DE
28 April 2021